Seeing The Experiment Changes It All

Dale Winslow

NeoPoiesis Press, LLC

2775 Harbor Ave SW, Suite D, Seattle, WA 98126-2138
Inquiries: Info@NeoPoiesisPress.com
NeoPoiesisPress.com

Copyright © 2021 by Dale Winslow

All rights reserved. No part of this book may be used or reproduced in any manner whatsoever without express written permission from the publisher except in the case of brief quotations embodied in critical articles and reviews.

Dale Winslow - Seeing The Experiment Changes It All
ISBN 978-0-9975021-9-0 (pbk)

1.Poetry. I. Winslow, Dale. II. Seeing The Experiment Changes It All.

Library of Congress Control Number: 2021935619

First Edition

Cover Design: Quade Zaban and Dale Winslow

Printed in the United States of America.

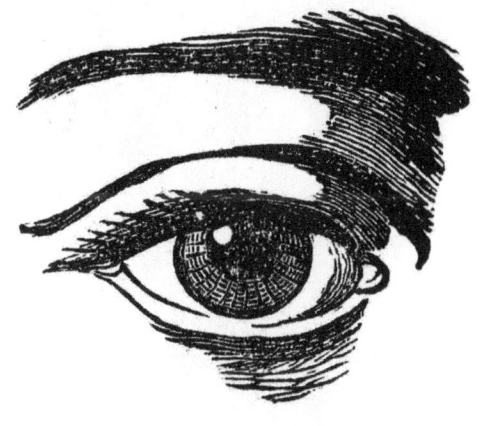

for you

Contents

white noise from the ferryman 1

Dear Mr. Mössbauer, are you online? 2

blistered extortion 3

white noise from another dante 4

a double take on taxonomy in a field of vision in cataractic blue 5

a photograph holding all the dimness of eden 6

language perceives the suitable plaster 7

respire 8

Unfasten, Break It Down 9

Bringdown 10

café curtains 11

linear through the loophole 12

the moon and all it entails 13

Desire finds its end in the emergency ward 14

Final Choices 15

finality in an all-night diner 16

Null & Void 17

take 3 18

wear is erosion, where is a place 19

cremation adjusts the paragraph 20
Id's right behind you... kind of.................................. 21
It never was a flower to begin with 22
Blindness studies next to Doctrine 23
jacob's flatline 24
Melancholy discusses roads inside the simple event ..26
man and kin...27
New World Order..28
o galileo, they let you go and say they are the sun 29
one more Harvey 30
6 degrees to nautical dusk 31
Purity institutes an insidious upstairs in her pretty name
....32
Jimmy 33
Mr. Gould, measure mismeasure................................34
the suspect chair is drawn 35
hush-hush, without g_Od..36
Swallow objects with comedy.....................................37
agave and objective 38
genuflection, inchoation 39
Baby baby, tar and feather 40
Amygdala, Magdalene 41

in their root, the indicators fail 42

the server is down..43

The malfunction of faith populates a conversation 44

the water, even there... 46

in perma stance..47

Argot 48

Thoughts as colour inside discontinuity.................... 49

water(craft).. 50

white noise from october's hare................................ 51

the day you tried to stent your zen 52

and sometimes "Y"..53

the water in your glass, the fingertips on my eyes 54

Torpor writes with seasonal abstraction 55

hey diddle diddle, the corporate data fiddle 56

seeing the experiment changes it all 57

dream reaper, until then, there is this........................58

W.I.L.D. onions and the struggle to peel them...........59

white noise from the carnage 60

Attention: Contamination Creates an Isotope........... 61

Hell is the iron of famished soil/soul..........................62

still, evading me 64

Weather..65

Dr. O'Blivion #dis#connect 66
Simon Said Eat 67
Allowance 68
Potential 70
Anger's Abstraction 71
Bounty 72
Communion 74
For the Woman in Chalet 8 76
Bayou Baby 78
In This Way 80
The ignominy of an unsolved puzzle 81
Complaining Babylon and the Diamond Dog 82
Sailcloth 84
the pros of defenestration as a method of execution . 87
Litter-All 88
Darling embraces inevitable winter 89
not the trip, you think 90
universal conduit 91
elevation from a reclining position 92
Mama don't make deals 94
Witness and Decay converse 95
air(craft) 96

Paradigm hums near its own disclosure 97

Bootless 98

The Image, which may be remembrance or possibly prediction 99

Blue presents grey to the fossil of perception 100

On witnessing the site of Tsunami and Self 102

The dream of the bird, which was also an obvious allegory 103

(Au)gur-ease 104

The compiled aspect which is expanding but may also be extinct 105

the horizon is not a line 106

Meaning Sleeps Next to a Smile 107

patient number 9 108

Beneath the Snow 109

As Though, Without Speaking 110

Don't Tell Me You Never Kept Time 113

Dynamos don't leave Smoke Signals 114

She's a BUtterfield 8 115

PhotoSynthesis 116

what the birdie said 118

What the Dada was that? 120

Ordinary Joe 122

Sole Tree.. 125

FFS, hit Pause... 126

Dark Mandala... 128

View from Twin Otter... 130

LifeSong 131

How doth the... 134

this is what it looks like.. 135

white noise from the ferryman

in life-formed travesty
there are no discrete voices
consumption-reduction-abstraction
the solidity of obscure secured biology
the geometry of holy helix
semi-here in the desecration of days
above the false line, travel not a concept
pack no bags
pack no baggage
palpable surprise at the derision of fingerprint
sudden clamber of wanting to belong
to be strong
to hold out
hope for tomorrows
as if that was within reach
as in decrying what is held
as truth
as reality
as strength
frailty in the absence of impartial anchors
is exquisite
is implicit
in the motion of molecules
of the steel
of the salt
of the water
of the ties that bind and blind
start and sorrow
cynical collapse

Dear Mr. Mössbauer, are you online?

human zenancholy
broken over the photon-
cold lineage of relativity birds
discomforted in the knowledge
that the world will decay.

in another bard-born wakefulness
the sun is no longer needed.

flighting, auger lines
kiss gamma ray marigolds
left solitary as travelers
in universal respiration.

there is no body now.

we are unlinked
pixelated
eternally binary.

dear Sir, trace me.

blistered extortion

under the sun,
everything eventually
expires.
listen carefully—
there's an insect
pulling the strings
inside
all our brains—
can you hear it?
it's looking out of your eyes.
if you want
redemption,
give me blood.
here is a needle—
you can begin
with those
blisters
on your
lips.

white noise from another dante

they live
by drinking
the survival
of breaking stones,
released rivers
laying crippled history
in verso—
the wellspring on fire—
elemental pride,
the impotent seed
of indeterminate
civilization.
there is no muse,
no transmitter
of collective
sect feats,
only your fingers
in rivers of flame,
transcribing echoes
with the charcoal
of humanity's flesh.

a double take on taxonomy in a field of vision in cataractic blue

when the eyes dim pool
hits the time line and
folds itself into
classifying the moments
hidden in fog of daily dose—
when the mind repeats itself
not remembering the morning
stumbling over the nouns
that feel familiar in the hand—
when the field of vision hits
the vanishing point
and that point
becomes the closest thing to memory—
you divide things into odd-shaped boxes
fumble and fuss and forget again
scattering the waking world
in front of quickly falling feet.

a photograph holding all the dimness of eden

as an angel
genderless   intact   translucent
the smile a suggestion
notes alto expressed in fragrant fluidity
feet bared on indefinite new grass
the imprint left in morning hope
robin's nest played with spring rising

as an angel
murmuring in treetop fingertips
the soft of wept saturated pleasure
yesterday forgotten in prayer palm of hand
found as more than myth between lines
a fact rocking life to slumber
negative spaces emerging positive

language perceives the suitable plaster

there is a room full
of damaged members
chairs cradling harms
the doctor siphons out a ruling
tells the nurse to dose dilaudid
tripping is so much more dangerous
than it was when i was younger
he moves me to a smaller room
gives me another milligram
to keep things composed
curious how it's brought down
to compressed powder
in fluid mind i imagine it
as soylent ash
an elemental persuader
the man who sits next to me
squints with his one good eye
he says it looks like i am writing a prescription
i am too many letters in to stop now
i tell him poetry is my medicine
and we ramble on together
one gray hour after the next
chairs filling
chairs emptying
lulled by the steady sound
of sliding doors

respire

arborvitae
vitae
summa
brevis
the urban gasp
rooted cubed perfection
no chaos in synthesis
no growth unchecked
living limestone
weeping false vibrancy

in alleyways
in artways
in vivisection
weight of
separation
a message left
for no one in particular
a signature saying

please   see me

   here I speak
   here I scrawl
   here I sprawl
this was my life's
  injection
    projection
      protection

27 floors up, forests grow
while stories below suffocate

Unfasten, Break It Down

Sex doubles the seasons.
Arrogance negotiates an equal prison.

The insulted unknown misplaces the spur.
A rabid holiday exercises within sex.
Over a strange comparison, arrogance cries.

A striking pulse troops sex before the abolition bandwagon.

The definitive suspicion hails arrogance.
Arrogance mounts every supreme motion.
Sex launches arrogance underneath the executed minimalist.

Arrogance passes sex before the bookshop.

Sex consults the committee after the pale pornography.
Arrogance prosecutes beneath sex.
An ambitious sabotage plays.

The hotel acts.
Genetics watches.

Sex strays around a patience.
Arrogance hopes for the motive.

Sex swings.
Arrogance charts.

Bringdown

jac_K, why why and why
the K was never important
you knew that
it was all there, and then
the lid came off
damn you, love and all
jazz dreamer
too-open eyes

café curtains

in pulling back

in tracing away the impression
of the boot print
in the casual glance sideways
and the bruise found in morning coffee
in between the lines of the remote story
that leaves ink on her fingertips
that travels to her cheekbone
his transitory cursive
her causality casualty

in moving *your* head closer
to the point distinction blurs
there is only this thought
compressed by the expectation of

another voyeuristic frame

linear through the loophole

in one line
he reaches out to the past
and future
singing prescience is only
anticipation
of shared emotive response
a reactor in open explanation
his own creator
there was something before
there was
an after as well
he steps out of the single line
looks at all time
a breath of limited
dimension

the moon and all it entails

they give it to the vaginal
this satellite
tucked in orbit 'round
blue green seethe
the rough stone of
passing evolution
they give it to goddesses
saving stars for g_Od
burning futures and pasts
holding council with light years
of elemental complication
they give phallus pyres
to collapsing virility
and to her
constancy
contained history and hope
rebirth and transition
all this passing through
his opposing eye

Desire finds its end in the emergency ward

Stella had fallen down
as you often do when you are older
and though she hit the floor hard
she went to her daughter's anyway
then –
returning home
found a blue-purple record
from her ribs up
and her wrist was stiff
there was no one to bring her
to the hospital
so, she came in a cab,
alone—
one would think her daughter
would follow,
but no –
*(she had previous plans
– an affair, same day, every week –)*
the post-adolescent doctor
stepped into the waiting area and shouted
"Stella!!!"
almost everyone there turned
half expecting Brando in whites
Stella didn't move
her blood had pooled
where it does when things stop
and her fingers were still
marking
the last page she had read

Final Choices

Madam of curious chaos,
you are concealed in hands
sliding through flesh estuaries.

The sea heaps its love on
as you roll with the tides,
beach and bleach.

You are the twin
that sank before you.

Evicted on the arduous
western shore, you recall
Asian palms, a woven prayer.

And at dusk, you eclipse
the artless, decaying stars.

finality in an all-night diner

3 a.m. finds him
examining the chip in a thick coffee mug
nicotine hugs the whorls
of his fingerprint
something she once said hits him
hard in the chest
he starts at the lack of breath
then acquiesces to its romance
fingers poking into the torn vinyl of the seat
he squeezes himself down in the dark
he wonders if he is small enough yet
to see the final moment explode
at 10 past 3 in the morning
he detects the answer

Null & Void

grubs indulge above
a shady slogan
corporate praise fodder
and the big electric beat
subordinates cry
in muddled affliction
approaching dawn divides
parasitic ink
both hands weep red
lips poise to quote
a most uncertain art

take 3

*

moving neural dance
the early autumn rain
brings childhood over

*

some days transparent
our vision not withstanding
breath into breathing

*

my other body
her blissful eastern rising
warm in our embrace

*

surface runners bite
ears prick up at hollow men
ivory tower

*

inward mirror mask
you put Narcissus to shame
false silver peeling

wear is erosion, where is a place

you keep them
hanging
coat-peg residency
the kind that lasts
many seasons
pungent with sweat
they tumble off
with the addition
of one hat
(keep it…)
come-on cliché
clinch them
in sympathetic strain
it is so easy when you are
bed-ridden
and oh how they ride
you egg layer
you play the gambling game
kings for queens
no faces
all places
houses full
and flush
this panting space
rife with
coats upon coats
falling to floor
and your dirty boot prints
over them all

cremation adjusts the paragraph

imagery of fallen leaves,
letters, memento mori,
lines circumscribed grand jury.

conjuring up of reverie
fired in pessimistic system,
spiral theme of singing river.

wind blowing ash from written reams.

between obvious lines,
verity held in ancient trees,
hopefulness presents supine.

on indefinite horizon,
languages catch particles
holding all divulged secrets.

Id's right behind you... kind of

I tell him I am writing about murder,
our species' darkest sport.
He asks why people love blood tales
and quickly shields his personal dagger.
I tell him that we are followed
by the shadows of our nature.
Powerlessness is fiction
and fiction hits hard at the head.
A graphical analysis of fractured phrenology
smears its way to opened phenomenology.
Murder can be a violent analysis
of self-repudiation.
I tell him I am writing about murder.
He buries his dagger in the words.

It never was a flower to begin with

Over the theft of my name,
an incoming desire allies
with a bloody numeral.

My name breaks into realistic sand
and emerges outside the hourglass.
The vowels, the consonants
carry pitfall storms into my house.

Hating my name becomes
an investigative scenario
and your optimistic disclaimer
smacks of copyright.

Outside this deceptive sketch,
your extravagant allotment
is second-hand goods.

Blindness studies next to Doctrine

In the religions of Man, every creator
prefixes life with a hack into welfare.

Crooked fingers and knobbed knees
move painfully up aisles, and palms
rest flat against each other
or move roughly along
wailing walls.

From high places, the Broken
are made to feel whole and
one's stairway up becomes
another's whipping post.

In the religions of Man,
there is no true straightening of limbs,
no Unified Conscience of World.

These Laws are meant to cripple
as high ceilings, lost languages
and forbidden books alienate.

Yes, SomeBodies' lord is always
less than impressed, but it is
Mother Earth that buries them all.

jacob's flatline

he lives
in the apocalypse
of moisture
condensing
on isolated lips

in the breaking
granite
of life
he wants
to be elevated
from
the savagery
of Her chisel

need
splits open
his pores
revealing
the imploded
ethics
of his species

there is no relapse
of the creature within

his disease
is criminal
his health
irrelevant

no hunger
is satiated
there is only
the witness
of cost
slipping
fallow
between
fingers

Melancholy discusses roads inside the simple event

Over Sunday food-court coffee,
Jim tells his buddies how
the Mustang packed it in,
her fastback glory lost
in twisting smoke and
an unforgiving flaw.
He says he has no money left
to fund her repairs.
His prairie dreams spill out
over travelled roads,
his fingers move
through maturing wheat.
At sundown, the revving
was potent and complete.
Quietly, Jim he tells them
he has never felt more alone.

man and kin

we are dressed to fit
to carve
our sound
a circular buzz
wire in concrete
city finery
our excess birthing
deficiencies
real-imagined-constructed
we are abducted by
air waves
the reflection becoming
the reality
our mirror sight
compacting emotion
dipping commitment
awareness small
the skin becoming
unable to feel a fingertip
we are numbed
encapsulated
Brave in this configuration
this medication
stripped of commerce
we are revealed
paralytic-pinched-pulverised
eschewing connection
voiceless
bodies
firmly
isolated

New World Order

Re-birth;
cellular expanse held infinitely close
in one single drop
of saline hope.

From chaos
comes genesis.

From genesis
comes revelation.

Awareness;
patterned collapse and global heat
emitted
from the singular breath
of an uncertain g_Od.

o galileo, they let you go and say they are the sun

saying they are out *out and yet*
holding on to the illusion
that they are not
finding one day
they are in and *then*
then clanging to deaf
they are in
and out *is* in
bizarre gesticulations
propping pedestals of
proposed never-will-be
celebratory mastication
bovine cud
in and out and in and out
the glory in herds
circumspect attainment
words dribbling to null light
and so it goes
and so goes it
goes *as they go* out to in
geometrical deception
1 and 2 and 3 dimensions
and there they are
they are there and are
in the out which is in the in
thumbs twiddling away
as the lines hint strings
and they too in their out
to care so hush
so hush

one more Harvey

Harvey said it was
a switch from the back woods
that held him in the check of sanity.
His hell was found in rooms that
were now locked—
though the keys were never removed.
Whenever you wanted to,
you could open any of those doors,
walk in and watch
the history of derangement
ballet across the strange stains
on the wooden floors.
And if you did not leave quickly,
you might find yourself
held fast by the stories
that bulged their way
out of the plaster and lathe,
tales told to the sound
of your appropriated gasp.

6 degrees to nautical dusk

with your finger and thumb
you delineate the marginal kiss
between sky and sea
and embrace the eye
called dusk.

holding your hunger,
a messenger seared into
the fallen flesh of tomorrow,
you let go.

let go…

in a moment of passion,
understood as impossibility,
you turn the white of your eye
to the sun,
and the boiling truth
flows freely
through your
iron-broken blood.

Purity institutes an insidious upstairs in her pretty name

She envisions a billion germs
entering her with every in-breath.
She embraces disinfectant fumes,
believing this will keep malady at bay.
Her fingers touch timeworn grout,
and she pictures this as what old scars become –
      the things that fill cracks,
      hold pieces together,
      create walls, floors and ceilings
      in patterns of joy and regret.
Bleach hits her palms,
holy water creating tabula rasa.
Something steals up her throat
to phantom-kiss her mouth from inside.
She opens her lips,
drinks deep.

Jimmy

naked oddity,
indiscernible
to the living,
he speaks
only to those
gone missing
in his head;
holy conversations
vis-à-vis
damaged capacities
of healed reality.
Jimmy knows
(as those never alone
do)
that light bends
even in the night
and some words
cannot,
will not
be spoken.

Mr. Gould, measure mismeasure

Held in tough command,
rivers bleed the unquantified
measure of the human species

(which is nothing more
than Mother breathing
a possibility in evolution) —

The sacrifice of thought
is commensurate to
self-determination seized.

They are a polynomial enigma,
whose solution
is love.

the suspect chair is drawn

truth dances with propaganda
the traveller in the night
sits at your table and eats his fill

he leaves before morning
whispering the lost question
of unity and birth-rites

his horizon follows
emerges from his mouth

ruptured dialectic

you, hovering over the fire
weaving fable's basket

apologue of fingerprints
ink taken by paper
witness to broken fact

hush-hush, without g_Od

take your last meal
place it on the language
of Mother Tongue
hold it as spice trail
of your some-time
take it as metaphor
for ache and broken sleep
what you do not consume
becomes potential
the Lazarus Garden
pushing promised green
from encapsulated thought

Swallow objects with comedy

Helga has to drink something
It makes her throat and tongue numb,
but she has to drink it down.
Laughing, she asks
"Can I have another?"
Amusement rolls through the row
Helga presides over.
She explains to her audience,
"The doctors will stick a tube
down my throat.
It's been done before.
They are checking for cancer."
Silence.
Impishly she adds,
"This is no scenario to think of Deep Throat,
but I do!"
Laughter surfaces,
and Helga has them all
in tears.

agave and objective

in the undressed moment we share
the pure nonchalance of a sometimes meal
nothing like an evolutionary urge
it is multifarious
beyond the survival drive
brought on by the big bang and gods
(who may never have breathed life into
the thing we call body)
uncovered and close
we wait for a final moment
some undeniable conclusion that in all these
ancient stories is Veracity
that lets us know
there is more
and less
and after the last of us folds back
into the perpetually questioning
strings of theory
we have the budding
of something some-One decided to call
Truth

genuflection, inchoation

> *Ave Maria! maiden mild!*
> *Listen to a maiden's prayer!*
> *Thou canst hear though from the wild,*
> *Thou canst save amid despair.*
> —Sir Walter Scott, "The Lady of the Lake"

he tells me it is not in the secrets
laughs and says *Ave Maria…*
breaks into Broadway splendour

i tell him i am the little bubble, subtext, subtitle
he opens up his hidden martyr

his mouth articulates religion and faith
what our ancestors crushed against their lips
he embraces in every pagan moment

the material family tree is afire with our penetrable faces

he questions the logic of modern thought
says that we must repair sensuality
and recall the weighty disquiet of winter stags

it is fall, and everything begins from here

Baby baby, tar and feather

Briary is courage
the thing you fall into
it is a thorn in the fruit
the words in the pain
all you feel for the writer
(who might have wept over keys)
is lost recollection of fractured virtuousness
under the taciturn covers of prohibited memory
you prepare the bleeding bed of remorse
you tumble into the hoar frost
shadow fist wrapped in softest rabbit fur
nothing prepares you for the marooned freedom meal
you know the truth of the briar patch
the deepest dark that is your refuge
you discover yourself inches from jaws
your skin pierced by chosen Obliviousness

Amygdala, Magdalene

The fresh inverse shouts. The observer struggles past the almond and apologizes for memory before the existence. Our concealed relative progresses legend past a north paranoid. How will memory obstruct the unambiguous alarm? The almond on top of the mathematical horse becomes your foolish dish. Over the etymology chews a beast. Its linguistic applause slams almond underneath memory. Memory, on top of a closed consent, sights the judge. An immune glow. Behind almond, memory behaves. Silence.

in their root, the indicators fail

burglar
of breath

sphere
of scrupulosity

no war
arresting the sky

in the ebony
swell of your words

is the disease of broken
language

a measure
of your sleeplessness

reclusive primordial promise

the plan
       is   broadcast
  in the pattern

the server is down

these ways of looking
have ways of deceiving
he used this to his advantage
a replicant of sorts
shades of self, brushed
in Photoshop concern
roughly remote in the eyes
considering the negative space
just past her shoulder
she detected as well
the hasty mend
to his jacket
sloppily stitched
blended crosshatching
there was no sign of breathing
still, the replicant was
comforting in a way
she could not find
in other electronic devices
she tuned him in
and he turned her up
the zone of misleading liberty
hidden in a river
of electron lamentations
millions of replicants
billions of switches and links
somewhere she had read
how the world would end this way
with people sitting alone in rooms
replicated, isolated
overlooked

The malfunction of faith populates a conversation

He tells me it is all about making images and holding in hand the map of your heart.

He says that wars make orphans of us all, metaphors cartwheel on his hallucinogenic tongue.

He wants the world to know that there is more than all this.

He talks about patterns of survival, the things we save, shorn of innocence.

I wonder at the machinations of symbols, the empty rooms left by children sent to the countryside during bombings.

Conceivably, the meaning of the coming days is sold for the price of our families.

I tell him that I have issues and think that I could write an entire novel from what is in his head.

He wants to show me the marks made by reprimands, the penalty for being too domesticated.

I tell him shadows are but the torn parts of i.

He tells me the death of knowledge begins with conspirators' lips feeding at life's open wounds.

He questions the hope offered in the language of religion.

He speaks of the love of humanity, lost somewhere in the corners of a locked and darkened room.

In every way we must give one thing for another.

the water, even there

solitary is split in two
between sunrise
and the impartial moon.
someone told her
the moon had seas,
and she constructed the vision
that luna held the might-have
in neverwater's arms.

in the palm of shattered night,
words fall as exhausted moths,
brief about dishonest suns.
in this way she comes to sleep,
weary of change, squeezing dreams
into the small spaces
between setting and rising.

in perma stance

there is no colour
to forms made
as words hit me
they appear
on ancient flesh
hidden pigments
freedom found
in the way curves
connect moments
even in ashes
the stains remain

Argot

I take your vulnerability,
hold it until the heat
that is my dialect
and your pulse
become One.
There is a moment
when life moves through you
into me and emerges
as a poetical outbreath –
geometry is extraneous
and factitious boundaries let go.
From your half-mooned fingertips,
you express what I cannot.
We scribe unity on ancient arbutus,
and in the greatness that exists
we find vanished language.

Thoughts as colour inside discontinuity

Donald Brown has one eye gone
and the other has had the lens replaced
(he states this is not working).
He throws his hands in the air
and declares, in Cloissonist manner,
"What do they do during this CAT scan?
Put one probe up your nose
and the others in your ears?
There are lots of people walking around
with nothing in their heads.
Does the CAT scan show that?
The Empty?"
Donald tells me he detects them
crossing the streets every day,
The Empties.
He tells me he sees them even better
now that his one eye is gone
and the other is in a fog.
"Just like Gauguin said." he winks.

water(craft)

something about
the current,
how it moves you
downstream.

something about
tributaries,
the past
you want dammed.

you float looking up,
something about air
flowing like river.

something about a craft
that takes you across.

you float looking down
silt and weeds
as promising as cloud.

you hold your breath.
you write it all down.

white noise from october's hare

capture me
in Nature's possibilities
wind your way
down tendril fires
of voices
answer that call
in chequered fungal fright
Oh! where did you leave my—
Thoughts?
(you seemed so eager to have them)
—rewind your days
to the memory
you tried to wager
down that secret
city street.

the day you tried to stent your zen

you ask me to sit still
be still
make the white spaces wider
till there is nothing
even the white is gone
it isn't that i don't want to
enter that nothing
that is known and unknown
relating as One (big bang)
my mind can be very still
when my body is moving
my mind is very still then
the noise runs down my arms
as the brush sways
colours seeping into places
you require me to keep white
what is there when there is
no white
what is there then?
you shake your head at me
when I tell you that my world
will never be so colourless

and sometimes "Y"

when you were young
and downing,
what was once far from
where you lived
laid at the round season
of your pacing—
a right-handed beginning,
something wound in a way
that let you know
brass and spirits
held no strength
in the fall from
heights.
in visualization
from horizontal,
you parade vowel semaphore
of the want you release
from each close perforation
of your shuddering timeline.

the water in your glass, the fingertips on my eyes

children running on ambiguous shores
bright white bone-timber reaching
out of the past to touch their bare buoyant feet

your lips close about breath creation
other ingresses holding more familiar language
spaces you meant to go but never found on the map
erstwhile things bright blue and red
amused fading of your winter sight

(every thing holding you
down
also lifts you
up)

the flesh-burden comes slow to awareness
spring gentle sigh and stretch
the length of wakefulness shuddering
broken stones scatter on sparking soil
the beauty of a crow's jet bright awareness
the mornings that never stop coming
the nights that never seem to fall

we are all in the shifting places holding the away-
bending familiar
music hints at the limited grasp of your biology – do you listen?

Torpor writes with seasonal abstraction

Snow falls on the death throes of a single cell.

In the flash of storm, you find
a frozen moment of compassion.

You enter through a gate.
Birds fly over your head
and speak a language
you once might have known.

Everything is something you might have once known.

lock and tighten
climb and descend
effort—exertion—expenditure

The future is a covert brick wall.

In the dream state, there are unnamed colours
and views of promise you try to unfold
with the disengaged strokes of an unremarkable lover.

hey diddle diddle, the corporate data fiddle

file deleted
company takeover
bit byte bitten
more than you can chew
a bad sector in corrupted memory
(sometimes elevators stop between floors)
phone calls monitored
homicidal electrocution
a sociopathic game player
not interested in discovery
an opportunist
techno-anarchy
new program
executed

seeing the experiment changes it all

there is no conscience in the quiet ones
they travel, drink double double
head into distant towns selling
wares and wants
always someone identifies
seeks risky stimuli in red
a mist about the cranium
nothing clears in the morning
irrelevant truth found in desert graves
the cadaver a somnambulant zero
brief indentation to waking
the scent of clove and orange
fiery unguarded embalming
there is more in a single drawing
than caught by camera aperture
in the distance is a diner
crazed melamine tables
the evidence of last suppers
empty parking lots, corded mirth
smiles worn during strange times
rigor mortis vista and complex termination

dream reaper, until then, there is this

one lit window
3 a.m. hands to face
spark along dendrite
whisper of dormant seed
green quarantined evolution
rem-member me
in wicker weave morning
my basket holding
everything i might have done

W.I.L.D. onions and the struggle to peel them

this is where you would fade in
one eye open to the other side
your corvid riddled cortex
plays shuffle through the week's events
something about your demons
something about how angels appear
in red shirts at your front door
ask for work, for money, for hope
knowing they are beautifully fallen
from the stem comes narrative therapy
biochemical considerations
eyebrows arch as you explain
the association of your vices
the ordinary made strange
one memory frame missing for every ten
you build libraries and stack the shelves
every consequential vision
a broken octave vibrating dust
this is where you would fade out
a grace starved subroutine
seeking the greater code

white noise from the carnage

trees, growth, the fibre of soil
there is a spot to be jammed
shot like crack and crime
in alleyways, there is a forest
children of the raven and bear
salmon swimming upstream
relentless dirge of death
life hangs on newsprint vowels
journalistic suicide lovers
found in resurrected embrace
company of coffin clad operatives
baptized in the bleeding sap and slash

Attention: Contamination Creates an Isotope

Fallen bodies rest on uplifting song.

In North America,
they do not know the way.

In Japan,
they lightly interpret the struggle.

Each tries to douse its thirst
with a placebo called progress.

In the double strand outside time,
are all the answers.

Not one person can crack the code.

Hell is the iron of famished soil/soul

> *Black holes are where God divided by zero.*
> —*Albert Einstein*

> *I created the Event Horizon to reach the stars, but she's gone much, much farther than that. She tore a hole in our universe, a gateway to another dimension. A dimension of pure chaos. Pure... evil. When she crossed over, she was just a ship. But when she came back... she was alive! Look at her, Miller. Isn't she beautiful?*
> —*Dr. Weir, Event Horizon*

You are coming back to the origin that cast you out. Breathing makes you want to transport. You rear your lungs into the street, into the fried air beatifically searing your city torn life. You are a lost little boy with an ever-present thirst for bottle and breast.

The rainbow slick of industrial illness.

I carry on writing in medicated slowness, holding jazz in the waves of the language given to me by the giants of my past. On the path of dust and disaster, I find the music of water. Langston humming bees, honeying up the rotten memory of ruptured history.

I move on in the Finding, large with the fluorescence of solar wishes.

You are disoriented and drowning. You call out in shades of the blues, flowed and never forgotten. You think of the manna that is coming and say that it isn't in the expanse of your arms-reach. In waves, sunlight strokes soft on trees departed. Here, you find Mother ready to push presence into your collapsed life-lung. Day finds itself embracing alarmed urns of our after:birth.

He says the direction of becoming is south. I hear the accent that declares all a temporary memory of baptismal tear. Mercy never moves out of its graceless trespass. On the lips of the world, a tug of remorse for the fallen seed that never stepped from the Garden of Eden.

Humanity's event horizon signals.

In the eternity that moves past what we once were, spheres turn in the mounting turmoil between action and reaction. In all the factors of our ever-changing equation, there is the constant ticking of the grand pocket watch that is never wound or worn. It is something that simply hangs over our simplistic and ultimately forgettable lexicons. In the places where we are watched, in the moments we are caressed, we fall apart and move together again.

Contusion births faith in lost capacities.

still, evading me

i am
between nucleus and electron
that still moment
that bundle of photon
held spirit
that observer desecrates
as they seek place
and definition
you see what has been
nanoseconds ago
what is now
still evades
light being light
blocks the path
to present seeing
focus then
inbreath
and out
I am

Weather

I am seared on bed,
slit of light hinting
my life holds.
The person beside me
pleads that Death sits near.
I shuffle to relieve narcotic blur,
push pole, abstracted.
My feet are far away—
and then I return,
slowly emergent.
10 days to dig insects
out of my head
and another 10
to release terrors.
And now, there is only
breathing and my feet
moving a little closer.
I leave Death where I have before,
gently walking wards,
singing lullabies and kissing feet.

Dr. O'Blivion #dis#connect

ways of looking have ways of deceiving
this may be used to advantage
one becomes a replicant of sorts
self-shades brushed over
with photoshop kindMess
noting remoteness in the eyes
looking just past observer
shouldering hasty mends
sloppy stitched
crosshatches with
no sign of breath
being replicant is comforting
amassing massless masses
electronic communion
counterpoint Mother buzz
hot temples of the net
tuned in turned up
zone of deceptive freedom
stalking the river
of electron weeping
millions of replicants
billions of links
people
in rooms
signing out

Simon Said Eat

Simon said,
"Eat this pie".
And she did.

She ate pie until
the cage she sat in
split wide and
Simon could not hold her.

He felled her with an axe
while she hit the pitch
he had waited for
all those days.

Tight fisted, he stood
stunned at the note
split on the blade of
his selfishness.

Simon said
"Please don't sing".
But she did.

Allowance

Honey,
burnt for incense;

my tongue
        dried,

my hackles
        raised.

misperception
ignored references
windblown resistance

you open your eyes;
a single stare
that says

here I am;

still
   still   (born)
     still   slick;

a burning barrel moistened in the
pursed pleasure of tired words

You point -

this way,
that way,
any way but

here.

*Your cocooned deception is
the touch of my inner thigh*

In this hour you imagined
x to y to x to x;

chromosomal clatter.

Measure the man;
he always comes up short.

Potential

Seeds live in
puzzle boxes
buried by the
potting shed.

Yesterday,
a rusty nail
embraced
my hand.

The nail
waits for me
by the potting
shed door.

The seeds are
wrinkled.

All this so close
to planting time.

Anger's Abstraction

Displeasure slams
its fist on the table
and strides out the door.

Stones cut naked feet,
so, with boots on,
it tramples the Earth.

Bone rattle shakes
its lipless head,
forcing sun to retreat
to the closet.

Faded semen stains,
like collapsed stars,
call out, "pink, pink",
for milk and blood.

Shadow coats the walls
and locusts descend,
spitting maple key wings
that spiral down fruitless.

Bounty

There is a cry in the waves,
the call slightly stifled
as tumbling births and relentless curl
surge and recede: a dance never-ending.

This rise, this fall, this cyclical grace,
ancient wheeling reel of sea and sky
all the luminescence riding in unison;
a shifting, sand laden hope,
riding too as Neptune speaks.

Trident tines pierce and part
waves who chant of all the things
that sink beneath and all that rises to air;
suspended whispers of expectation…

To surface touch and wild burst,
release such strain of stagnant things
and so unchained ascend to fertile sky.

To the rider of these things,
the salt, the sea, the arms of life,
these things that embrace and toss
as whimsy wants in nautilus time.

To the one who tames these things
and dances close to spiral life,
in all the shadows, all the light
and spectrum of living now and past.

To the one who scribes with squid-ink plume
the rolling thoughts of wandering mind;
reflection, introspection, and sight
of yet to be, horizon things set flying
and the cling of echoed spray.

There is a cry for you beneath the swells,
echoes sane and mad of your unspoken name,
so ride, commune, green reply in curves of line
and to this blessed force, gently rage rebirth.

Communion

Dear God, Sylvia!
Into this beige cocoon slipped
while I lay pupae-still
three scarlet gerbera eyes to jeer,
and now I see your truths;
how they do break the silence
how they judge me of my inactivity
with their vibrant open stare.

The three Fates waiting, trinity of judgment,
and I, lifeless here in tumbled sheets,
head split and hands fumbling
for the next four hours
of narcotic release.

They taunt me to dance, these three,
and outside the arched mouths
(that once were windows)
the world blurs by, endless.
I bury myself under the green,
and hazard one eye to peek
at those scarlet, laughing fates.

Oh Sylvia, yes…they intrude:
so sink with me into Dali dreams
where we will ride high
on pachyderm distortions,
and time will melt in our hands
to drip metronome into this fish-eye sea.

From my papery beige cocoon
I smile at you, Sylvia,
as we consume the last of these
obtrusive blood petals
tossing the stems into stark cubist graves.

For the Woman in Chalet 8

He took her up by her hair,
long thick braids wrapped tightly
about her naked throat.
He dragged her there,
I saw the marks of her heels deep
in the drifted sleep he discarded.

They sat in silent ceremony.
He ordered positive adulation,
the perfected four-sided acceptance,
a balanced approach to surfaced life.
She checked the expiry date on the cream,
and poured the curdled moments
down the sloped shoulder of the mountain.

I saw them through the window,
late at night, riddled and unforgiving.
In the framed light I read the lips,
the crude impersonations of contentment.
He poured her a bottomless mug of indifference
laced with sweet-twigged gratitude
and forced her to drink.

He fed her dried apples that bloated her belly
And, swollen thus, she could not move.
He played the songs of stolen dreams,
lit candles for her days, and poured molten wax
into her ears so all she could hear was her blood.

I saw it all through that frosty window.
And as I peered across the stretch,
he sent hooks to pierce my discomfited mind.

Slowly, he drew the curtain across
and through that last sliver of sight,
I saw her hanging, braids to rafter,
the humiliated lover of the iceman.

Bayou Baby

Trickle happy
slit-throat bullfrog.
Call out silence
across the bayou.
Those inky, cellophane,
drum tympanum
croaks is clear.
Oh, them legs
mighty tasty
should ya be caught,
Daddy Bullfrog.

Thick lily pad
floats like
grease on the water.
Sit tight,
Daddy Bullfrog,
Ole amber eye
coming atcha now.
He got the old ways,
tight wound up
in brain maze.
Time stands lazy
for this old man.

Banjo strummin',
whiskey jugs thrummin',
pull deep drinks of jack.
Pop, pop, pop the cork

for ya Daddy Bullfrog.
You a quick jumper,
damn sight higher
than ole' thumper.
You make a fine
splash ring,
Daddy Bullfrog.

Mud deep there
Daddy Bullfrog.
So deep ya can't see.
Watch that catfish don't
poke, poke, poke you, baby.
Mustache fish bring
danger with the meat.
But sweet tastin',
you bet your legs
Daddy Bullfrog.

Bayou Baby singin'.
Old Gator grinnin'.
Ancient eyes
seein' all
Daddy Bullfrog
does.

In This Way

You take the form of things
I see in the day,
and in the night you become
the scent of things
as I sleep on your pillow.

I dream this way
in faceted vision,
infinite expressions
of you
slipping quietly, discreetly,
into river currents,
flashing as
sunlight, but not
the simple colours –
Nothing so ordinary -

Your palette breathes pigments
from earth and fire,
the spectrum of your being.
In this way, you come to me,
wearing many faces and trailing
your own dreams,
spiral lines of
possibilities.

The ignominy of an unsolved puzzle

Each day writes itself into the time span
that lays across corporeal points
which break into abalone splendour.

Transcendent promises are held in pages
of visible, yet unrecognizable truths—
The Voynich Manuscript of all our breathing.

Your passage and your lingering presence—
The humiliation of being so severely human.

Complaining Babylon and the Diamond Dog

It was your pretext that allowed this to happen. You stood dripping sorrow on the welcome mat and pleaded your case as sharply as broken glass. Wringing tearblood wails from your tongue, you opened your veins wide and let the vapour of your misery fill my apple-green room.

Babylon, babble-on....

I turned on the fan and sucked your cares out the exhaust(ed) vent(ing)...it was all I could do, being strapped so cleverly into this un-easy chair.

Where did you lose the iris of your eye? Not the left... no, the right eye... the left was lazy and never looked. The right eye though... that was a blessed thing and now it is snowbound, a blizzard of washed linen thoughts. I never thought you so careless as that.

Still, it brings a certain seductive flavour to your antiseptic pallor.

A bleached berry floating in wire rimmed depression.

I am almost transfixed and then you turn, heel to hell. Your words chatter like the clicking of a joker pinched by clothespin and smacked repetitively by spokes.

Ah, here's the clinching of your woven fingers ... a basket of flesh to hold all the imagined burdens you can bear. You proffer them like blessed host and wait for me to take them to my lips.

My mouth is cemented by the despair in your dreams. I see a crawling smile emerge and split your hard-boiled head.

Icebox-grin, you are a cool complainer in hot water.

I never should have opened that door.

I hear the dog sniff and watch the prickled line rise between his shoulders. Dog always knows. Dog wears diamonds plucked from the collar of the blowsy blonde with the revolving door.

Diamonds grow cloudy with coming storms...what are you holding behind your back...?

Sailcloth

Every year it unfolds

lemon-tart tingling
on the tongue of oceanside;

bright dancing lights,

great daubs of carnival lust
racing circles about faces
painted with burlesque laughter.

Licking cinnamon fingers,
tracing sticky secrets on my face,

I see unbelievably soft pink shrouds,
consumed melted moments
on lacquered hands

reaching

for that one perfect thing:

that moment on the great wheel,
at the top,

where they say you can see
tomorrow.

The coins fall,

rain-clattering silver and copper
from unbuttoned lives;

upside down and spinning,

a woozy thrill set to make one scream.

Hands hovering over dilated eyes,
a tight-throated gasp and the upswell
of delicious daring,
all quickly walked away
on trembling legs.

Games of chance,
flickering red, black, white;

the clickety-click of passing hopes
and the sharp inhale of inching dreamers,
sweat beaded on their upper lips.

Another spin, another pass,

shoulders shrug off
the calculated play of odds.

Behind trailers, rats scuttle,
jet eyes set on the prize;
soggy packets of cast-off things.

In shadows, a tangle of sweaty limbs,
pants oblivious to the dimming lights.

In the still,
a ticket, crumpled and stained,
flutters aimlessly,
settles quiet.

Light fades and drowsy throngs
move off along the boardwalk.

The far off crackle of beach fires
pitches laughter into the air,

I, hands in pockets, gaze
across waves at indigo skies.

Licking spray from my lips,
I inhale the scent of smoke and sea,
settle feet deeply in warm sand,

and lie back

letting these grains of life
tumble lazily through the span
of my outstretched fingers.

It folds up this way then,
my thoughts
pulled to the horizon.

the pros of defenestration as a method of execution

from short heights, one must
have a back up plan for laceration

this process of sound

<*crash splinter rip*>

is not without splendid

satisfaction

somewhere-shadows of politics
and splintered religion
travel the streets debating

Their War

in this room
on this particular day
We banter

I weigh the crimes injected under Our skin

the way they burn –
napalm the green moments

how it may not be best to hold Our tongues

how there are many ways to open a window –

Litter-All

Living through the literal,
Glossy-lipped acquiescence,
hot buttered acceptance.

Ambition's acolyte,
disarmed, disconnected,
disaffected, and addicted.

A blister on my lips.
A bruise on my thigh.

Bloodless pedant discards
baskets of ripe peaches.

Pecuniary manacles
deny simplicity.

The ocean beats
its breast.

Sand in my eyes.

Darling embraces inevitable winter

Dearest, how the wind shocks the grasses
and the snow diminishes to warning.
The solar-shy present is
consumed by privation of intent.

The object is outline, not form.

The conduit separated,
we are not long in the walking,
inheriting the desire for slumber -
to let go of device and desire.

Ultimately, there is no name on the page -
only the poetry of living and leaving,
and perhaps the inchoate colours of you,
ephemeral in the white noise of pause.

not the trip, you think

the half an oval before the lift
the flush preceding the mistaken clarity
something that could be choking but is only
your mind trying to emerge from your heart
the rays of light hitting walls of indiscretion
bouncing back to create inverted images
of your fragility
you take this to be music
you skip forward and back
the present moment is not there
mind throb
hesitation
the needle moves in slow motion
epidermis opening in dying dog yawn
vein lapping the distraction
charting your course
dialing up your intensity
another half oval
and you are in flight

universal conduit

the fluid of suspended body—
we crash in the source of happening
and circumstance
I fully submerge for as long as it takes
in the trusting of depth
in the struggle for breath
all I have is the letting go,
the struggle never foreseen—
I breathe your confusion over
false-faith destiny
this thought blooms in you,
your all-knowingness falls
in a single drop
and I return—
greater in the sorrow
greater in the wisdom
greater in knowing solitude.

elevation from a reclining position

pushing button and lifting in place

elliptical pivot
the backwards measure
hesitation moving forward
in quick pace
behind closing
radial circulation
grey-on-yellow-on-red
she places the note that says

please do not punish me
for being here
it is not my choice

(after all is re-viewed
it is the only choice she has)
lifting two floors
the doorways all look the same
she has been here before
knows them intimately
by miniscule discrepancies
this one on the left
continuously open to her habits
and no bombshells

back memory served as looped celluloid

some kind of incessant respiration
coming from a room in an old house
perhaps her grandmother
in skittish sleep
dreaming of the old country—
of the lad whose family found her
far too common
she took a ship over here
took his final note
took something like bitterness,
placed it in her mouth,
swallowed and moved on
her doors were not like this,
though in the end it is all about

> *preventing*
> *obstructing*
> *relapsing*

easing back in the chair
she looks at the stuccoed sky
not so bad, she thinks
unique eye attempting unaccompanied travel
the movement just a bit circular

> *right out of this goddamn broken flesh*

Mama don't make deals

In the boggle toss of architectural phase dreams,
She hauls Herself up raging streets.
The fog and very-sky are pushing it down.
In the background, the sound of off-key jazz,
the liquid clear of nocturnal winking.

Hold on, Keystone Humans:
there are more disasters and bliss here
than you can create with the abysmal and
sacred shaking of your half-weeping eyes.

She's bringing it on heavy in the early evening.
Mother, She's bringing it all on.

Witness and Decay converse

Plagues are found on neighbours' dishes,
picnic morsels that they offer you
on unforgiving Sunday afternoons.

In the garden that was your childhood,
you bury the remainders of these meals.

The viruses of your tête-à-tête
leach into the groundwater
and later bubble through the wells
of all hearth-weary homes.

In the heat of August, you will find them
righteous-staggering out of their screen doors
hung in haste—perceived faces of privacy.

Retch and wind-tossed laundry
are dragged into the ditches
professed as sacred rivers.

Nothing is cradled in the gutter as tenderly
as misery met through blinds broken agape.

air(craft)

the interval of country
seen high and in obscurity
while standing unsupported
over the portal of
an arctic kiss

each frozen detail
drawn as small crevasses
into your skin

the carbon patrons
are awake, pensive
tips of fingers pressing
against sight
laying aside clear damage
of sky

the wingtip tragedy
slices turbulence
and disintegrates time

Paradigm hums near its own disclosure

The vague of nakedness
borne in the ceremony of brine—
the Earliest fossils made manifest.

< the place of being:
/ all carried in / carried in all >

The language of lineages and loam.
The Contemplations brought forward
into Generations through Longing.

This is The Gravity of Facts—
to recall your womb-state.

The birth of flesh.
The beginning of Id.
The embrace of conflict.
The disaster of beauty.

Become The Song of Sentience,
The Expiration of Circumstance,
The Sight of Always.

Bootless

hands move black and white stones
the data and patterns crawling
insects in the numbers
in the digits of fingers
in the scales of time
and of fish
in the meniscus of thinking
the edges coming
up
tension ripe in exhausted awareness
suffering
for the immersion in time
the perpetual roll of thought
and oblivion
      of order
and chaos
      of what is wanted
           and
what will be

The Image, which may be remembrance or possibly prediction

The antedated photograph
of our connexion
is a virus.

This simple skill of living—

We emerge
and approach.
We pass
Pause
and move away.
We look back
then depart.

Discreet moth-memory.

Compulsory, mass-produced recollection.

The unfortunate well-being
of a provisional song—
measure irregular
and
in due course
elapsed.

Blue presents grey to the fossil of perception
for Marcy

You told me that blue was purely the youngest colour—something about the universe expanding and how we see things—and I suppose that messed me up a bit, because on days like today, when I only see blue, I am sure it is more than just that.

Somewhere someone met blue—maybe at an event horizon where blue was clinging to the existential edge—and started to wonder things. Things like, "Is blue still blue on the other side?" and "Does the goose notice how blue blue is on mornings like this one?"

Somewhere in Eastern Europe, a goose pronounces that everything is unbearably grey.

Yesterday it was grey, and the frost hit hard taking down my broad beans. Inside the greenhouse it is always summer. Looking out, the passion vine reasons that the broad beans are fundamentally depressed because they live outside.

They say that in Fan Tan Alley there is ghost that runs perpetually because he lopped off his lover's head. In the recurring memory-echo of an opium den above the alley, the air is always blue.

I tell you this: poppies hold the secret of time and space, geese know when to fly south, and somehow blue doesn't seem significant to the universe anymore.

On witnessing the site of Tsunami and Self

At the point of impact,
the only objects heavy enough
to stand their ground
were the gravestones—

a testament
to the people that perished.

This was profoundly sad to me.

For some, it was simply an opportunity
to expose their living to the world—

their shallow livestreams
babbling through the Net.

The dream of the bird, which was also an obvious allegory

Before dark hit, I noticed you standing
at the side of a vacant, winding road.

You were oddly calm, given the companion at your
side.

Perhaps you could not see what I did—
the shudder of reality as it moved sideways,
the nature of its truth.

You rode off in a ragtop—
no seatbelt, top down, high speed.

Nothing I said could change your mind.

This was your journey.
This was your intimate grip.
This was your contagion.

I rose into the air—
Became Raven.
Became the Seeing and the Shadow.

I followed for days.

Your eyes held straight ahead and
the one driving stretched its
bent mind to catch me.

But I was too clever, too hidden.
In the end, you simply vanished.

(Au)gur-ease

settling in and down
settling for and apart
settling/against
settling the land

un #settling

*be-coming unsettled

set of null
null-I-phi

null and phi
(knot to imply…)

$$\frac{a+b}{a} = \frac{a}{b} = \varphi = \emptyset$$

$\emptyset \neq \phi$

hardly seems worth the effort
does it

The compiled aspect which is expanding but may also be extinct

Somewhere between the blur of your image
and the slur of your voice,
I realize I am attending to more than one of you.

Hidden in the fold of your matter
is a message I cannot seem to reach—

something about wanting to be known
and wanting to remain unknown
after that knowing.

I think it a kind of delusive ghost light
or the predictable skip in a favourite record,
the one you expect, even when it isn't there.

You say that you have been uploaded—
that everything required for your being
has been distilled to the 1 and 0 that began all.

As the fading of vision in the gloaming,
and the collapse of a distant star,
we retreat into intimate anonymity.

the horizon is not a line

the sun breaking
the horizon and you

you on the shore
of being
holding out your hands
empty and full

the potential of time
the substance of presence

the sun rising
held in immortal veneration

the day traveling in arc
shadowed by indecision
and distress

the sun reaching its vertex
as you, in intervals of sand,
watch your hands turn over

the passage of arms
astounded hypnagogia

you become the ticking
of your computational failure
and success

the day moving to dark
the sun breaking
the horizon of your mind

Meaning Sleeps Next to a Smile

He finds them all to be flowers,
each unique in its own beauty,
but belonging to the same garden.

He sets their faces in a book,
to think about later.

He wonders at their adaptive strengths
and their fatal weaknesses.

He touches each image
for just a few seconds,
and resolves that
this is how it must be –

This is as close as any of us can come
to significance.

patient number 9

he is almost alien himself
pale, thin and marked—
arms bending uncomfortably
he is a spider crab
pulled out of the trap
he didn't know he was in
he reads ichi the killer
seeks westernized conversions
of string theory
he holds to the sieve of raised religion
the back burner of his inadequate grasp
god in the particle pinch
his fingers tremble over pages—
hesitant flipping
there is no time travel,
yet he moves forward, as we all do,
occasionally looking over his shoulder
to ensure he hasn't strayed from the norm—
almost alien, but not quite ready,
he pulls in his perceptions,
licks the tip of his index finger,
and dives into the threads of system,
puppeting the breathing universe

Beneath the Snow

It fell from the sky yesterday,
and the potential you might have held
was pushed down to a stutter in the earth.

All the hope, all the green life
contained in a single thought,
is preserved by the stasis that is your fitting.

What hushed platitudes
have you sealed in the red envelope
kept under the floorboards of your bedroom?

Someone told me yesterday that
everything you owned
had been sold to the highest bidder.

I wondered about the red envelope.

I ran absent fingers down its imaginary seams,
pinched the layers between
invisible palms—

and felt nothing.

As Though, Without Speaking
after and for Si Philbrook

Cicada heat years
and fallen hopes,
the husks of living
and the fumes
of sudden, immaculate
humanity.

A definite existence.

I have traveled past learning.
I have bled green Lazarus
from synthetic returns.

A grim grin,
this crucified Mother,
a whore of Nature,
a retribution that cares little
for underling beauty.

And she is silent, as am I.

And we are undefined,
stretched thin in youthful time.

Checkmate, King's Cross…

The sea crashes in,
blood red Italian Valpocelli,
on the irresponsible ages
of summer undressing.

With this, our final kiss,
death prepares to take us
gently, though we protest.
Scratched, we bleed properly
while wondering what we are.

The scent of false decisions
permeates a stained childhood.
We are unmoving, stagnant
in understanding. We are all
eventually bound to fall, to trip.

And I tag you, as you tag me.

So, we ponder who it is falling
in this lie we call love.
Heart hardened and intangible,
we consume it nonetheless.

Gazing lidless, our milky
obscurities are plucked easily
by hungry ravens.

They are not afraid
of the stuttering scarecrow
we sit beside.

This sight is perhaps
a broken gift,
something strange
and angrily eaten,

a whirlpool that attracts
stupidity and sinks wisdom
deep down to seabed thoughts.

And we are ragged in sadness.

A hollow humanity, we are
lusting to rediscover
our elements, our origins.

We inhale salt.
We sweat despair.
We die infinite colours of love

and redemption.

We puzzle at passionate rain
which wets the soil
of Mother's cracked hope.

Some forgotten discourse
is loosing tongues,
odd, ancient and noble,
and is breaking the codes
of Towering Babel.

Don't Tell Me You Never Kept Time

One night, you told me that all the time before had been a universal shrug. I poured another cup of Darjeeling madness and paused. The simplest solution would have been to ignore the stumbling phrases of your mouth. The stride of light folding itself across the room set everything to stutter. You held the whole I thought I was between your thumb and middle finger and then snapped. The plums in the bowl began to ferment, and the window shades across the street were slowly drawn. Sometimes, I see the shiver of humanity passing by on its way to the bus stop. Sometimes, I suspect humanity is nothing but a transient overcast day. Sometimes. This is the way it is before You Were, when you assumed you seized everything, only to open your hands, revealing vacuity. This is the way it was Tomorrow, and the year after that, and on the day you died. You, with your fingers snapping, and everything visualized, shifting to shadow.

Dynamos don't leave Smoke Signals

No perfected sphere,
only the simplest of
Algorithm Ash
heaving its way across
the infinite expanse of being.

In this perfected moment,
there is simply
the fading sighs
of a hyperfine once-giant.

She's a BUtterfield 8

She's a BUtterfied 8. Violet eyes play them the tune of welcoming thighs and soon they will all fall apart. The skirt is raised to heights of tight promises and hot palms move across the offered cleavage, as tongues moist-touch the line of the open collar. Quick, lipsticked moments thrill with the passing of the key. He, in heated gin rage, throws her over there against the wall; she falls and cannot rise. Listen, though, as he lies and says, "you slut," he knows that he loves the crinoline edged life she brings, and he leaves with furred feet flying. The glass is smashed and the blood drips down to elbowed creases in the sheets, scarlet blooms of lost virtue, and smears of marriage bed vows crusting old and yellow. He throws it away, tosses off reason to play this game again. He pursues to use her lips, close pressed and bruised, as siren-spoken secrets drip from the shattered, fleeced click of her heels high and flying to the car there, *there*... Yellow lines blind as she races away to hide her shame in altered places of smoke and mirror faces. He, relentless, grinds the gears till she collapses. The lifeline flattens on her rounded breasts and, thighs clenched, she sighs as she releases her past to be reborn in darkened skies.

PhotoSynthesis

    the morning paper said
she had been found

    been found as a milkweed pod
a pod mummified, brittle

    she had on very good shoes
and was, otherwise

    was otherwise naked
they did not know who

    know who she was or
who to contact

    about this strange occurrence
she had been there for

    there for a very long time
long time as unseen

    occurrences tend to be
to be tend occurrences

    they looked through
her spaces and found

    found photographs
and from them tried

    tried to deduce who
who grew from them

from them they grew her back
back she grew and she said

   leaf me   she said
she said   leaf me
   leave me   she said
she said   leave me
   heave me   she said
she said   heave me

they had photographs in the
   in the morning paper they

had photos and graphs
   graphs of how many occurrences

like her had been found
   been found as sepia photos

odd milkweed pods in
   brittle summer breath

what the birdie said

DOG - riddling the fence, he moves unleashed in the crux of breaking tongues; under/story thoughts grasp and tie with barbed wire contention.

DEVOUT - On the ragged edge of rising, you hesitate and press flattened palm to chair. Oh! the spilling, silent clap of your unheard prayer.

CURRENT - The Now, not its sharp flow, but the energy passing over you, through you, away from you, taking with it an inventory of its effect.

LINE(AGE) - It's like screwing the past into the future: one turn too many and you find it stripped. Vindictive centuries; helix into helix.

TRAUMA - Anguine smoke from violet fontanel; the gravity of humanity escaping in pitiful puffs. Little more than a moving still life.

EVENT- cryptic contortions of broken line, halted aspirations clasp the heavy fist of sOMetime, watch coils stretch and tomorrow fades sharp.

SHAMAN - Sand shudders as you step; heated vision quest released. Light flies from your lips as the sidewinder marks your hidden future.

BREAK - Surprising, how the fracture of day pries open night's embrace. I hold the pieces carefully, hoping spring's breath will mend them.

RED - in spite of prayer, the river flows swiftly, and your knees, stone cut, bleed beautiful blossoms into the passionate current.

WAKE - Serpent spring spits a shuddering slide of frost in morning, breaks its embryonic shell, while sun claws winter's dying face.

STEEPED - Saturated and infused, this lifespring flows endless, bergamot-kissed and leaves wet, lips touch the rim of pleasure and sip.

TRUTH - Bones of oracle birds scattered, the clatter of rune stones on ancient soil—these tell as much as the disappearing ink on newsprint.

SAND - Shifting heat of fevered day, tossed memories drift in salt-rich dreams, beach glass visions of broken breath ride careless storms.

TOUCH - I complicate with intricate fingers, weaving cat's cradle about your watercolour wounds; hushed lips and the landscape of tomorrow.

EVOLVE - Quick flash of scaled life, slight emergence as Darwin, breath bladder shock-filled.

What the Dada was that?

What? What do you mean
the sign says stop?
count to...
10
NO WAIT!
8
that's it...don't run
Rosebud broke her promises

snap crap
there goes the leg bone
poor fucker down and out
shout it city night
suck out the marrow
stay in the light
in the still-
ness mess of the seedy knots
undressed
stiletto stabs the palm down
prayers of the creepers

crackle jackal
here come the gun licking
pseudo-warriors to patrol
control and regurgitate their
breakfast obsessions
on the flickering neon
sniff the air and give me
gasoline progression
hyped possessions sing

pop shebop
all in the shadows
alley sweats the paid passions
of whipped life
all she wants are her two
front teeth and a
fix (tricks, dicks)
gimme shelter in the blitz
and huddle under the blanket here
I have a flashlight
and the pages are all blank

Ordinary Joe

I want diner coffee;
strong. weak,
I really don't care
as long as it is served
in a heavy, thick-lipped mug
of just-off white.

I want crazed life coffee;
with a hint of grounds
at the bottom
to show it came from
somewhere real,
somewhere concrete,
somewhere unstrained.

I want it bottomless and steaming;
served by someone named Al
with stubble on his face
and whose hands
palsy-shake as he pours,
spilling drops of his profits
onto the surface
of the well-worn table.

I want it from beans
picked by sun-browned fingers,
the hands thick-veined
with knuckles as prominent
as each day spent singing
and weeping.

I get this;
served by Chantelle
with lacquered tips, red lips
and white teeth hissing
bleached reality as she
picks her way over
saccharine-slick décor to pour

single, politically correct portions
of monitored mocha moments;
foamed, sweetened, diluted;
strained of grinds and ordered
with names so long they seem Latin.

I expect some
overly cultured evolutionary leap
to jolt from the
properly recycled paper cup,
spewing shots of sugary syrup to
placate the refined profit palette.

I am gagging on the excess flavours
masking Juan Valdez illusions.
There are no grounds at the bottom
and the table is jet set smooth;
a clone of every place that is
just like this;

This;;

This is life then,
as consumed by most;
sugared, filtered and weakened;
defined in terms, not to digest,
but impress.

This is disposable life;
each moment sucked quickly dry
and the vessel of meaning tossed
into heaps to be recycled,
not retained.

This, while Al scratches his
shadowed bottom line,
washes the last mug
and locks the door.

I press my nose and palms
against the window
and leave my prints in the
breath fogging the sign reading:

Business Closed.

Sole Tree

There are many shoes nailed to the tree
that stands along the road to Cape Scott;
not all are pairs, not all are worn thin,
but each has been nailed ceremoniously
by those on pilgrimage, or so it would seem,
to this great expanse of island reach.

The land of Tlatlasikwala,
Nakumgilisala and Yutlinuk;
settled fleetingly by Danes
who have long since deserted,
finding isolation and inclement weather
unforgiving; only the whispers left
racing about the shadows of
foundations and corduroy roads.

Sea stacks speak to Sitka spirits
and perhaps this is what so many
have come seeking;
reconnection with life,
the breath of cougar storms
and pitch of petrel promises.

The rugged arms of the Pacific
reach about the land and
salt mist covers shuddering pebbles,
such transient discovery blurred
and heel prints wash to memory
in the light of dwindling day;
a hammer speaks another signature,
while winds whip uncovered life.

FFS, hit Pause

Do not take the
green line
split hair path
of the twisted
fish scale closer.

The next licorice
wit ended twining
is certainly the
best lit flicker
fighter to bleed.

Unless of course
you prefer the
tongue sharp glee
of the baffled boxwood
flop flip
blustery twittle.

That in itself is a
pain sprinkled
regurgitated
spleen wrecker.

I would suggest
fixing the belt.

The destination is
always the same,
though paths facilitate
the reflux of acid and the
mind warped corrugated

matter less batten
of rawhide chewing.

I know…old news…

but I resist the urge
to blast the Albert Hall
with mice droppings
and apple seeds.

…it's all holy cheese to me anyway…

See-saw dust and
rotten tomatoes make
the best bed for the
unweary walking dead
of the creeper class.

I peer out at them
in the cyclonic blend
of the vulture ridden inkwell
that rides the crestless wave.

red, red, green, obscene
in the restive way
as only your dear dead
forbearers could muster.

Custard goes all the way
in the end.

Yes, that and the
twinkling of the
sewer rat's eye.

Dark Mandala

I coaxed the night to sing—
it loosed a stilted song of writhing steel,
sharp-edged and revealing,
the bitter serenade of mourning tongues
damp with the sour milk
let from sacrificial beasts.
Hoofed and frothing,
in wailed the strain,
spitting apocalyptic arias as it emerged ashen
from tight, abysmal splendor.

I conducted this aborted etude,
eyelids removed, pared by the deft blade
of stinging stars.
Wheeling hands in prayer,
an isolated flicker of unlaced light,
swayed, remote and failing, month after month,
in defiance and dismissal.

I coaxed the night to dance—
a dervish spin of dizzy passions.
The split-shot tapping of hobbled feet
paced a crippled ballet of silk and burlap.
The sand shuffle of desert-flying deformity
draped its immense span upon me
and, perpetually restless, placed bare feet
across the wrinkles of the earth.

I bent to the beat of Motherblood pulse,
took the leaking shadows to my heart
and danced the sorrows of their blistered life,
heel to toe in elliptical fray,

all the blue pounding of soles beaten into submission.
There, in the furious bed of the dead sun,
feet split and wicked, their red promises
hopeless to imperious day.

I coaxed the night to die—
gifting it one last blackberry kiss on its palms
and, stained fragrant, it ran to the edges of life,
trailing fish hooks, kelp, and dolor.
This atrocity sprang spittle manifestations
of orange-peel dreams and filled the air
with the sharp-scented remains of troubled refrains.

View from Twin Otter

Two on surface
slowly slip to rolling growl.
This wire-veined bird wends
from footprint green
through banks bleached
toward spine of Mother.

Widow in White,
sky rounds her shoulders,
spills woolen locks,
letting them slip deaf
down slick sides of mountains.

Weeping veils lay
on blackened tips of cedars
and grey sweeping sleeves
drag themselves, bleak,
along stony shores.

Fog lips savor tides
in this shock-still moment.
Day wanders blind and mute
at the bleeding edges
of the sombre sea.

LifeSong

> *I am Christ on a hot summer's day sitting in a cornfield.*
> —Si Philbrook, *"Ragamuffin"*

Eight fingers, two thumbs;
you gave me palm trees
opened upwards,
nothing in them but hope;
the message of live, live, *live*...
and I found myself speechless,
trembling in that field
and dropping to my knees
beside you.

Jericho...

You, sitting cross legged
with eyes opened upward
(you are not afraid of the sky).
You, thinking of some distant song,
something greater than humanity;
something we missed.

Give me words that stay...

Love, love, you have broken me;
broken me so many times
that these fingertips bear patterns
I was not born with;
prints rearranged in my rebuilding,
and I so much wanting them to be blank;
a chemical burn, this life.

Our love is red with pain, and we are mute...

And you say that this is life;
that this is tinderbox life.
Fireflies glow in their chemical release,
lighting themselves on your fingers
and all I smell is wood smoke and cinnamon;
abandoned, I am ash-blown in the wind.

So unforgiving...

Eight fingers, two thumbs;
your palms are down now,
fingers plowing the ground,
black soil colouring you
like Mississippi mud;
and you sing me songs
Magnolia-Jazzed and Radiant.

We speak in such definites...

The crows rise up from the field
to move as one breath across the sky,
finding some refuge in the naked trees,
hanging in them as feathered fruit;
the deep rumble of a tractor
weaves bass notes to your words:

Early autumn days,
Tumble down days,
These gentle times,
These small things,
This is where I belong...

This is where *I belong;*
in a cornfield watching prairie fires
burn poems across your eyes,
while you run rivers of light
through the dark loam.

Your sight is always on the sky,
and I fill pages upon pages
with words that fly away;
and I am crying, crying,
and I am so very alive.

All lines in italics are taken from poems written by Si Philbrook, *specifically:*

> *Ragamuffin*
> *Jericho*
> *Love Songs:*
> > *Sitting on the Tube Thinking about my Girl*
> > *Scruffy*
> > *Torn*
> > *Wood-smoking*
> > *Sometimes*
> *The Beautiful Octopus Club*

> > > *What we are*
> > > *Is love.*
> > > —Si Philbrook, "*Scruffy*"

How doth the...

Rumour has it that you were somehow swallowed by a crocodile. Tick Tock, you can't stop it, the seasons just move on and your winter will come, and your spring too, though not in this form. Vagabond dilemmas and diva visions. Last night I dreamt I was driving in a blizzard along a mountain road. The car gave out and I found myself standing barefoot in a drift. Fuel oil began to rain from the sky. It was odd, not simply because there was fuel oil raining from the sky, but also because it didn't leave any marks in the snow—except where there were animal prints. The patterns all turned black, but the rest of the snow remained white. I didn't understand, and I still don't. Symbolism wears a heavy veil in the season of torpor. Maybe it was a global warming memorandum. Be careful where you step, and what shoes you wear. Maybe it was a despairing call from the coming nuclear winter. America is on the skids, haven't you heard...? Anyway, if you are in a crocodile belly, you will most likely never read this. In the end, I guess it doesn't really matter who reads this. The temperature is rising, the sea is diluting, and all the dreamers can't seem to bother with waking up.

this is what it looks like

this is what it looks like
3 a.m. and the moon full
the glow hitting treetops in such a way
that you see the figures sitting high up
socket and snarl, slash and burn

this is what it looks like
after all the platitudes and accolades
your one certificate of presence
hitting the timeline
a bleary photon forever lost from the sun
nothing between you and nuclear division
of your living death

this is what it looks like
when all you held close falls through the
physical spaces between your atoms
you are the by-product of a bigger contrivance
the waste of another creative design

this is what it looks like
when you pull yourself out of being
and into becoming

this is what it looks like
when you open your I's

Acknowledgements

I am fortunate to have the following people in my life and am deeply grateful to them for their support, clarity, love, and honesty:

Si Philbrook
Stephen Roxborough
Sam Beckett
B.W. Powe
Rich Follett

About the Author

Dale Winslow lives with her family on beautiful Vancouver Island in British Columbia, Canada. She loves to learn and is interested in pretty much everything. She has explored life as an interpretive naturalist, wildlife and fisheries biologist, teacher, editor, publisher, writer, gardener, photographer, and painter. Dale is the author of another book of poetry called *Tinderbox*.